GLADYS AYLWARD

Missionary to China

Written by
Shannon Armstrong

Illustrated by
Shannon Armstrong

Gladys Aylward was small for her age, but that didn't keep her from much. She had a strong spirit, and was very determined.

At the age of fourteen, Gladys became a parlor maid to a wealthy family who lived nearby. While she worked at this fancy home, Gladys saw many nice things.

All of these nice things made Gladys wonder... "Will fancy clothes and yummy food make me happy forever?" Gladys couldn't help but think "I must be missing something!"

One day, a friend invited Gladys to church.

While she was there, she met a stranger

who told her all about God's love.

He told her how Christ died for her, and loved her

even though she would often do bad things.

Gladys knew that this was what she was missing!

She asked Jesus to come into her heart,

and told the Lord that she wanted to serve Him

with her whole life.

She would often pray " God, here's my Bible, here's

my money, here's me! Use me, God!"

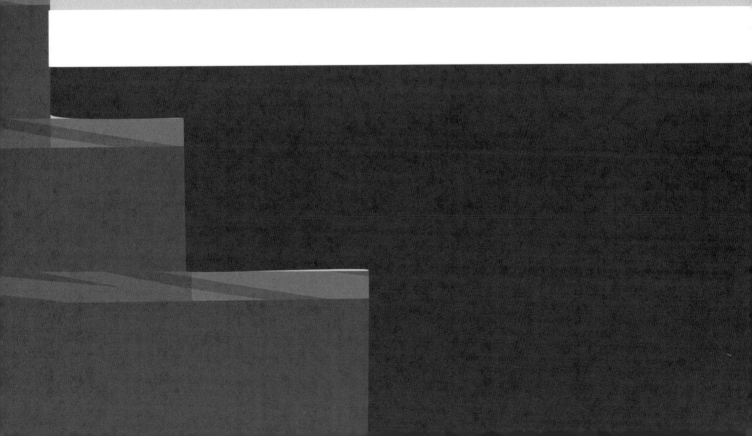

Every day when Gladys would go to work, she
would clean the fancy library at the fancy house.
When she finished cleaning, she would read all
the different kinds of books.

One day, Gladys found a book all about China! This
made Gladys want to go to China very much.
She began reading every book on China she
could find.

As the years passed, Gladys' love for China grew and grew. She had read about the Chinese people, and how they did not know about God. This made Gladys very sad. She wanted to find a way to get to China and tell the Chinese people all about Jesus!

Gladys began saving her money so she could buy a train ticket to China.

LONDON

ATLANTIC
OCEAN

INDIAN
OCEAN

After many years of working hard and saving money,
Gladys finally had enough money to purchase a train ticket!
She said goodbye to her friends and family, and boarded
the train at the Liverpool street station.

CHINA

Gladys knew that the money she had saved for so long was only enough to get her to China, and wasn't enough to bring her back. She would need to trust the Lord.

She boarded the train, and over many days, crossed over Russia, and arrived in China.

Gladys was finally in Yancheng!

She knew she would need to work hard to learn the language
of the Chinese people. Gladys moved in with a missionary
who had lived in China for many years. The missionary taught
her many things, and Gladys was very thankful for her.

Finally, Gladys knew the language well enough to speak with the Chinese people! Gladys began traveling to small villages all over China. As she traveled, Gladys learned many new things from the Chinese people. The villagers would share special recipes with Gladys, or teach her special crafts like **zhezhi**. (Paper folding!)

 As Gladys got to know the village people, she began to share stories from the Bible. She would tell them the good news, that Jesus loved them so much, he died on the cross to save them from their sins!

Many of the villagers asked God to forgive them of their sins after hearing these Bible stories from Gladys!

But soon a fight broke out between China
and Japan. Many people told Gladys
that it was too dangerous for her to
keep traveling to different villages.
They told her to return home to London.
But Gladys loved the Chinese people very
much. She knew that God would protect her,
and show her what she should do next.
So Gladys stayed.

One day, as Gladys traveled to a nearby
village, she found a small child
who did not have a Mother or Father.
Gladys decided she would take care of her. She
did all she could to make sure the girl was safe and fed.

But everywhere Gladys went, she would find more and more children who did not have a Mom or Dad to take care of them. Gladys knew that with God's help, she could be the one to love them and care for them! So Gladys kept helping them...

One, two, three, four, five, six, seven children!

Eight, nine ten, eleven...

At one time, Gladys had more than one hundred children

in her care!

The more Gladys' family grew, the more she knew they were not safe. The fight between China and Japan made living in China very dangerous.
Many people were looking for Gladys.
She knew she had to get these children to safety.

Gladys packed everything she had, and told the children to get ready for a long trip. It would take them twelve days to walk through mountains and rivers to get to safety.

The next day, Gladys and the children began their long walk over the mountains, across the Yellow River, and into southern China.

Their journey was hard. Gladys and the children needed to trust God to keep them safe. Sometimes at night, it would get very very cold, and they had no place to sleep. But they continued to trust God.

After walking for many days, they came to the Yellow River.

Gladys did not know how they would get across.

There were no boats, and the river was very wide.

Gladys and the children began praying, and singing to God.

A man with a boat heard their singing, and came to see what

all the noise was about. "I will help you!" He said.

Gladys knew that the Lord had answered their prayers!

At last, they arrived in southern China!
God protected them!

Gladys had become very sick from the long trip.
She knew she needed to take time to rest.

Even while Gladys was sick, she thought
of China, and how much she loved the Chinese
people. She thought about all the ways God had
protected her and her children.

"Maybe one day" she thought, "I will return to China"

...And she did.

LET'S TALK ABOUT IT!

Q: "Why did Gladys want to go to China?

Q: "Do you think Gladys was ever scared?"
"What can we do when we are afraid?"

Q: "Do people in China still need to Hear About jesus today?"

Q: "Do YOU KNOW ANY MISSIONARIES LIVING IN CHINA?"

Q: "How can we pray for our missionaries?"

Memory Verse: Psalm 56:3

"What time I am afraid, I will trust in thee"

Make your own
Almond Cookies

1/2 c butter, softened to room temp.	1/4 cup sugar
1 egg yolk	1/2 tsp baking soda
1/4 tsp. almond extract	16 whole almonds
1 cup cake flour	egg wash: 1 tbsp egg liquid, + 1 tbsp water
2/3 cup almond flour	
1 small pinch of salt	

Instructions:

In a large mixing bowl, Cream butter with egg yolk, sugar, and almond extract. Set aside.

In a separate mixing bowl, shift salt, cake flour, almond flour and baking soda together.

Combine all ingredients together, and knead into a dough.

Cover and refrigerate for one hour.

Preheat oven to 350 degrees

Form dough into 16 small round balls. flatten slightly.

Decorate with one whole almond in the center.

Brush with egg wash.

Bake for 18-20 minutes, or until golden brown on the edges.

Remove and let cool.

Follow the instructions below to make a paper boat!

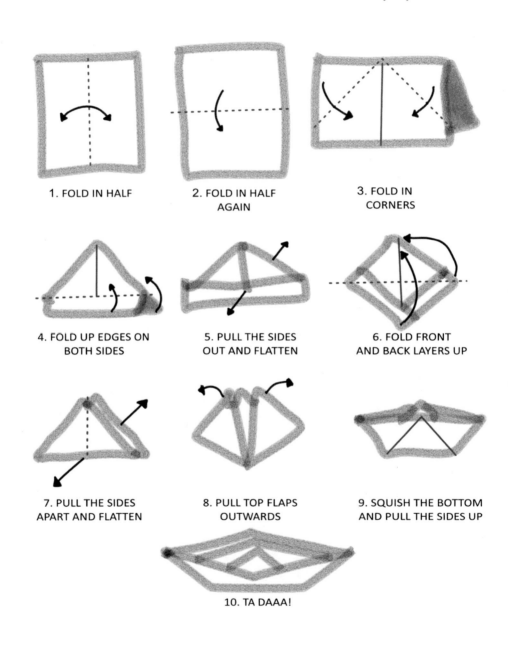

1. FOLD IN HALF

2. FOLD IN HALF AGAIN

3. FOLD IN CORNERS

4. FOLD UP EDGES ON BOTH SIDES

5. PULL THE SIDES OUT AND FLATTEN

6. FOLD FRONT AND BACK LAYERS UP

7. PULL THE SIDES APART AND FLATTEN

8. PULL TOP FLAPS OUTWARDS

9. SQUISH THE BOTTOM AND PULL THE SIDES UP

10. TA DAAA!

Send a letter to a Missionary on the next page!

Dear _____

Today, I learned about China!

I learned that _____
_____
_____
_____
_____
_____
_____
_____

Love,

Made in the USA
Las Vegas, NV
24 May 2023

72495235R00026